~Introducing Fiqh Series
Vol.7

Introducing the *Fiqh* of Marital Intimacy
(المقاصد الصالحة في فقه المعاشرة)

Written and compiled by
SAFARUK Z. CHOWDHURY

AD-DUHA
LONDON 2008

©Ad-Duha, London 2012

First edition 2008

Updated Edition 2010

An educational publication from Ad-Duha London
Third Floor, 42 Fieldgate Street
London E1 1ES
E: info@duha.org.uk
W: www.duha.org.uk
T: 07891 421 925

─── Imam Ibn al-Jawzi remarked:

"It may be that sex produces offspring the caliber of al-Shafi'i and Ahmad Ibn Hanbal. If that be so, this is better than a thousand years of voluntary worship…"

ورب جماع حدث منه ولد مثل الشافعي وأحمد بن حنبل فكان خيرا من عبادة ألف سنة (إبن الجوزي، تلبيس إبليس ص 358)

Contents Page

Section:	Page
Table of Abbreviations	5
Table of Symbols	5
§1. Introduction	6-8
§2. The Reward for Marital Intimacy	9-11
§3. Foreplay	12-38
§4. Oral Sex	39-42
§5. Sexual Intercourse	43-55
§6. Sex and Menstruation	56-60
§7. Anal Sex	61-62
§8. Miscellaneous Rulings	63-65
§9. Conclusion	66-67
Appendix: Etiquettes of the Wedding Night	68-72
Key References	73-76

TABLE OF ABBREVIATIONS

Art.	= article
Bk.	= book
pp.	= pages
ʾ	= the Arabic letter ع
ʿ	= the Arabic letter ء
‍.ا ه	= 'end of quote' where a cited textual segment in Arabic ends.
s:	= additional comments made by the translator

TABLE OF SYMBOLS

#	= *hadith* number
(…)	= contains transliteration of Arabic terms
[…]	= contains additions by the translator
… / […]	= ellipsis where a textual segment is elided and omitted in translation by the translator
{…}	= enclosure of a Qur'anic verse in translation
§	= section

"*Beyond the Veil*: The *Fiqh* of Intimate Relations"

الحمد لله حمداً يبلغ رضاه وصلى الله على أشرف من اجتباه وعلى من صاحبه ووالاه وسلم تسليماً لا يدرك منتهاه.

——— ♦ ———

§.1 Introduction

- Islam is not averse to anything that enhances the love, desire, attraction and fulfillment between couples.[1]

- It recognizes the natural need for one partner to enjoy the other and recognizes too that there are different levels and dimensions of gratification and pleasure beyond simply the act of penetration and singular climax.[2]

- The experience of sex within an Islamic marriage is often perceived merely as advantageous and reflective of the husband's priorities and needs to the exclusion of the wife's but this is grossly inaccurate.

- Islamic rulings on this point of sexual gratification are replete with the requirement for harmony and balance through effective and mutual fulfillment – one partner enriching the physical needs of the other and not diminishing it.[3]

---

[1] S. Z. Chowdhury, *Introducing the Fiqh of Marriage and Divorce* (vol.6), pp.47-48.
[2] Ibid., pp.48-51.
[3] Ibid., pp.52-59.

- Below will be basic and brief outlines on key areas of sexual conduct between spouses and its ethics from the Islamic perspective which include the following five topics:

    1. The reward for being physically intimate.

    2. Foreplay.

    3. Oral sex.

    4. Sexual Intercourse.

    5. Menstruation and Sex.

    6. Anal Sex.

    7. Miscellaneous Rulings.

    8. Appendix: Etiquettes of the Wedding Night.

- This is an expanded section made into a separate volume from *Introducing the Fiqh of Marriage and Divorce* book which is part of the Ad-Duha educational publication series. Most of the rulings discussed and mentioned are taken from the Hanafi legal manuals. There are, however, a number of contemporary books written by scholars and educators in the field which are very useful and helpful for those investigating and learning this particular area of Law.[4] Ideally,

---

[4] See for example: R. W. Maqsood, *Muslim Marriage Guide*, pp.83-107; Bk. 12, part 2, §3. in *On Marriage* (trans. by M. Abdus Salam from Imam al-Ghazali's *Alchemy of Happiness*);

this present book is for classroom purposes where the material is explained under the guidance of a teacher; nevertheless, it will still be a useful reference for those pursuing studies individually or merely researching the topic out of general interest. The book is supplemented with additional materials such as PPT slides, interactive contents, further notes and comparative discussions which are not included here but available on the structured course the book accompanies. It is hoped that there is benefit for the reader in this separate volume and we ask Allah to accept the humble effort as a small service to His *din*. Amin.

Love and Sex in Islam, part 2, ed. by M. R. Muhametov and L. But which is a collection of various *fatawa* on marital issues and sex in Islam; H. Hartford, *Islamic Marriage*, pp.130-140; M. al-Jibaly, *Closer than a Garment* and Ibn Adam al-Kawthari, *Islamic Guide to Sexual Relations*, pp.7-34.

§2. THE REWARD *for* MARITAL INTIMACY

It was narrated from the great companion Abu Dharr (ra) that some people from among the companions of the Prophet (saw) said to the Prophet: 'O Messenger of Allah, the rich people will get more reward. They pray as we pray and they fast as we fast, but they give in charity from their extra wealth.' He (saw) said: **"Has not Allah given you things with which you can give charity? Every *tasbiha* [s: saying *Subhan Allah* ('Glory be to Allah!')] is a charity. Every *takbira* [s: saying *Allahu akbar* ('Allah is Most Great')] is a charity. Every *Tahmida* [s: saying *al-hamdu lillah* ('praise be to Allah') is a charity. Every *tahlila* [s: saying *la ilaha illa Allah* ('there is no deity but Allah')] is a charity. Commanding right is a charity and forbidding wrong is a charity. Having intercourse [s: with one's wife] is a charity."** They said: 'O Messenger of Allah, if one of us fulfills his desire, is there reward in that?' He replied: **"Do you not see that if he does it in an unlawful way he will have the burden of sin? So if he does it in a lawful way, he will have a reward for that."**[5]

عن أبي ذر : " أن ناسا من أصحاب النبي صلى الله عليه وسلم قالوا للنبي صلى الله عليه وسلم يا رسول الله ذهب أهل الدثور بالأجور يصلون كما نصلي ويصومون كما نصوم ويتصدقون بفضول أموالهم، قال : أو ليس قد جعل الله لكم ما تصدقون، إن بكل تسبيحة صدقة ، وكل تكبيرة صدقة ، وكل تحميدة صدقة، وكل تهليله صدقة، وأمر بالمعروف صدقة، ونهي عن منكر صدقة، وفي بُضع أحدكم صدقة ، قالوا : يا رسول الله أيأتي أحدُنا شهوتَه ويكون له فيها أجر؟ قال

---

[5] Muslim, *Sahih* (#1674).

: أرأيتم لو وضعها في حرام أكان عليه فيها وزر؟ فكذلك إذا وضعها في الحلال كان له أجر"

- Imam al-Nawawi (d. 676/1277) explains this narration as follows:

"His (saw) phrase: **"having intercourse is a charity"** – with the *damma* on the letter ب – may mean 'intercourse', or it may refer to the private part itself [...] And in this is an indication that permissible actions (*al-mubahat*) may become acts of worship if there is a sincere intention. Intercourse may become an act of worship if the intention behind it is to fulfill the rights of one's wife, or to treat her kindly as enjoined by Allah Most High, or to seek a righteous child, or to keep oneself or one's wife chaste, or to prevent both partners from looking towards or thinking of unlawful things and other good intentions (*al-maqasid al-saliha*)..."[6]

قوله صلى الله عليه وسلم " وفي بُضع أحدكم صدقة " : هو بضم الباء، ويطلق على الجماع، ويطلق على الفرج نفسه ... و في هذا دليل على أن المباحات تصير طاعات بالنيات الصادقات، فالجماع يكون عبادة إذا نوى به قضاء حق الزوجة ومعاشرتها بالمعروف الذي أمر الله تعالى به أو طلب ولد صالح أو إعفاف نفسه أو إعفاف الزوجة ومنعهما جميعا من النظر إلى حرام أو الفكر فيه أو الهم به أو غير ذلك من المقاصد الصالحة قوله قالوا يا رسول الله أيأتي أحدنا شهوته ويكون له فيها أجر . (النووي، شرح صحيح مسلم ج 7 ص 92)

---

[6] al-Nawawi, *Sharh Sahih Muslim*, 7:92.

Thus:

1. Sex is highly virtuous in Islam – it is a rewarded act.

2. Our blessed Prophet (saw) approved of sex when the intention is right.

3. Intention (*niyya*) elevates an action into an act of worship.

4. Sex is a means of chastity within a valid legal marriage.

§3. FOREPALY

- There are many details and particulars related to foreplay, its types, benefits and positive impact on the long-term health and experience of a marriage but what follow in these sections is only the basic rulings (*ahkam*) within selected types of foreplay acts as well as general remarks.

- Foreplay (*mula'iba* / ملاعبة): is any act that arouses desire for sexual activity in the partner. Foreplay is generally of two types:

[1] *physical* (touching, caressing, fondling, sucking, etc.) and

[2] *verbal* (compliments, amorous exchange of words, etc.). Islam permits both types.

- The Prophet (saw) made direct references to intimate psychological and physical acts between spouses which are meant to create and increase sexual arousal, in anticipation of sexual intercourse.

- The noble Companion Sayyiduna Jabir ibn 'Abd Allah (ra) narrates:

"The Messenger of Allah (saw) asked me: **have you married? I replied: Yes. He asked: Virgin or non-virgin? I said: a non-virgin. He then asked: why not a virgin so that you can play with her and she**

can play with you (*tula'ibuha wa tula'ibuka*)."[7]

قال لي رسول الله صلى الله عليه وسلم أتزوجت قلت نعم قال بكرا أم ثيبا فقلت ثيبا قال أفلا بكر تلاعبها وتلاعبك...

- Another narration states:

"[...] every game a Muslim plays is futile except for archery, training one's horse and playing with one's wife (*mula'abatahu ahlahu*) for they are from the true and praiseworthy acts."[8]

---

[7] Narrated from Jabir b. 'Abd Allah by Bukhari (#2967) and Muslim (#715) in their *Sahihs*. The wording of this version is from Abu Dawud in his *Sunan* (#2048). Cf. also al-Haythami, *Majma' al-Zawa'id*, 4:257.

[8] Narrated from 'Abd Allah ibn 'Abd al-Rahman by Tirmidhi in his *Sunan* (#1637) as well as Abu Dawud (#2513), Nasa'i (#3580) and Ibn Majah (#2811) in their *Sunan*; Ahmad in his *Musnad*, 4/146; al-Mubarakfuri, *Tuhfat al-Ahwadhi*, 5:19; al-'Iraqi, *Haml al-Asfar fi'l-Asfar* (his sourcing and grading of hadith in the *Ihya'*) on the margins of al-Ghazzali's *Ihya' 'Ulum al-Din*, 2:353; al-Hafiz Ibn Hajar al-'Asqalani, *Hidayat al-Ruwat*, 4:30 and al-Shawkani, *Nayl al-Awtar*, 8:247. See also Ibn Hazm's *al-Muhalla*, 9:55 and al-Albani, *Silsilat al-Ahadith al-Sahiha* (#315) as well as his *Ghayat al-Maram* (#389) for another version from 'Ata' ibn Abi Rabah with a rigorously authenticated transmission (*sahih isnad*) that reads:

"**Anything that does not have the remembrance of Allah (Mighty and Exalted) is futile or heedlessness except four things:**

كل شيء ليس من ذكر الله عز وجل فهو لغو و لهو أو سهو إلا من أربع خصال : مشي الرجل بين غرضين، وتأديبه فرسه، و ملاعبته أهله، و تعلم السباحة...

[1] a person walking between two targets;

[2] looking after his horse;

[3] playing with his wife and

[4] learning to swim."

إن الله ليدخل بالسهم الواحد ثلاثة الجنة صانعه يحتسب في صنعته الخير والرامي به والممد به وقال ارموا واركبوا ولأن ترموا أحب إلي من أن تركبوا كل ما يلهو به الرجل المسلم باطل إلا رميه بقوسه وتأديبه فرسه وملاعبته أهله فإنهن من الحق...

"[…] and then there is a report where it states: **whenever anyone of you has sex with his wife, let them not be naked like wild asses, i.e. like donkeys but begin with mutual intimacy through words and kisses**. The Messenger of Allah (saw) said: **None of you should approach his wife like an animal. Let there be amongst you a 'messenger'. He was asked: what is this 'Messenger' here? He replied: kisses and words…**"[9]

---

[9] al-Ghazzali, *Ihya' 'Ulum al-Din* with the commentary of al-Zabidi entitled *Ithaf al-Sadat al-Muttaqin*, 6:175. This narration from Anas (= al-Daylami, *Musnad al-Firdaws*, 2:55) has weakness in it as stated by al-'Iraqi in his *takhrij* of the *Ihya'*:

| "…hadith: **"when you have sex with your wives, do not be naked like wild assess"**. Ibn Majah reported this *hadith* from 'Utba b. 'Abd with a weak channel of transmission." | حديث إذا جامع أحدكم امرأته فلا يتجردان تجرد العيرين أخرجه ابن ماجة من حديث عتبة بن عبد بسند ضعيف. |
| "…hadith: **"do not approach your wives like animals."** Abu Mansur al-Daylami mentions this in his *Musnad al-Firdaws* from Anas and it is *munkar* (rejected)." | حديث ولا يقعن أحدكم على امرأته كما تقع البهيمة الحديث رواه أبو منصور الديلمي في مسند الفردوس من حديث أنس وهو منكر. |

وفي الخبر إذا جامع أحدكم أهله فلا يتجردان تجرد العيرين أي الحمارين وليقدم التلطف بالكلام والتقبيل قال صلى الله عليه وسلم (لا يقعن أحدكم على امرأته كما تقع البهيمة وليكن بينهما رسول) قيل وما الرسول يا رسول الله قال (القبلة والكلام) _ (الغزالي، الإحياء علوم الدين جـ 6 ص 175 مع إتحاف السادات المتقين للزبيدي).

- These texts thus indicate a strong encouragement for amorous play between couples before actual sexual intercourse (al-jima').

- A remark on a preliminary: it is permitted for spouses to engage in foreplay with their clothes on and indeed without their clothes.

- The permissibility of kissing, cuddling, fondling, caressing, rubbing, embracing, gazing at each other (al-nazar), enticing and erotically teasing with clothes on is clearly permitted. The same ruling also applies to spouses when they are completely naked.[10] This is based on the following evidences:

Hadith 1: "Guard your nakedness ('awra) except from your wife or what your right hand possesses…"[11]

---

[10] See H. A. Shu'aysha', *Tuhfat al-'Arus wa Bahjat al-Nufus*, pp.182-188.
[11] See the narration of Mu'awiya ibn Hayda al-Qushayri by Abu Dawud (#4016) and Tirmidhi (#2794) in their *Sunan*; Ibn Daqiq al-'Id, *al-Ilmam bi-Ahadith al-Ahkam*, 1:14; Ibn Taymiyya, *Majmu' al-Fatawa*, 21:337f; Ibn al-Qayyim al-Jawziyya,

احفظ عورتك إلا من زوجتك أو ما ملكت يمينك...

Hadith 2: "Allah has indeed made [women] a garment for you and made you [men] a garment for them. My wives see my nakedness and I see theirs..."[12]

إن الله تعالى جعلها لك لباسا، و جعلك لها لباسا، و أهلي يرون عورتي، و أنا أرى ذلك منهم

Hadith 3: "From Sa'd b. Mas'ud al-Laythi who said that: 'Uthman b. Maz'un came to the Messenger of Allah (saw) and said: 'Messenger of Allah, I feel embarrassed that my wife sees my nakedness ('*awra*).' [The Messenger of Allah] said: **'why when Allah has made you a garment for them and made them a garment for you?'** he said: 'I dislike it'. [The Messenger of Allah] then said: **'they see that of me and I see that of them'**..."[13]

وعن سعد بن مسعود الليثي قال: أتى عثمان بن مظعون رسول الله صلى الله عليه وسلم فقال: يا رسول الله أني أستحي أن يرى أهلي عورتي . قال: "ولم وقد جعلك الله لهن لباساً وجعلهن لك لباساً؟" قال: أكره ذلك. قال: "فإنهم يرونه

Tahdhib al-Sunan (on the Margins of *'Awn al-Ma'bud*), 11:56; al-Hafiz Ibn Hajar al-'Asqalani, *Hidayat al-Ruwat*, 3:254 and his *Taghliq al-Ta'liq*, 2:159 and Ibn al-Qattan in his *al-Nazr fi Ahkam al-Nazar bi-Hasat al-Basr*, p.94.

[12] This version is found in the *Musnad* of al-Harith ibn Abi Usama, p.116 and Ibn Sa'd in his *al-Tabaqat al-Kubra*, 3:394 and is deemed weak.

[13] See 'Abd al-Razzaq in his *Musannaf*, 6:85 and al-Tabarani in *al-Mu'jam al-Kabir*, 9:37. The narration has weakness in it due to the transmitter Yahya b. al-'Ala' who is rejected (*matruk*). See al-Haythami, *Majma' al-Zawa'id*, 4:66-172 (#7561).

مني وأراه منهم" قال: أنت رسول الله؟ قال: "أنا" قال: "أنت فمن بعدك إذاً؟

[قال]: فلما أدبر عثمان قال رسول الله صلى الله عليه وسلم: "إن ابن مظعون

لحيي ستير..."

- In the Hanafi manual of *fiqh* entitled *al-Hidaya* by the great jurist al-Marghinani (d. 593/1197), it states:

"Regarding his statement (**and a man looking at the private parts of his lawful slave-girl and his wife**). And this is an absolute ruling on looking at their entire body whether with or without desire. The basis of this is the statement of [the Prophet] upon him be peace, **"lower your gaze except for your servant-girls and your wives"**. And because above that it is permitted to touch and embrace, then it follows that looking is even more worthy of being permitted. However, it is preferred that each person not gaze at the nakedness of h/her spouse due to the words [of the Prophet] upon he be blessings and peace **"when one of you approaches his wife, he should cover as much as he is able and should not be naked like wild donkeys"**[14] [...] And Sayyiduna ibn 'Umar (ra) would say: 'it is better to look [s: at the private parts of his wife during sex] as it is the optimum way of achieving gratification'."[15]

---

[14] Ibn Majah, *Sunan* (#1921). This narration has weakness in it according to Ibn al-Qattan, *Ahkam al-Nazar*, p.125; see al-'Iraqi in *Haml al-Asfar* (cf. al-Zabidi's *Ithaf al-Sadat al-Muttaqin*, 6:175); al-Hafiz ibn Hajar al-'Asqalani, *Mukhtasar Zawa'id Musnad al-Bazzar*, 1:579 and al-Haythami, *Majma' al-Zawa'id*, 4:296. See also al-Bayhaqi, *Sunan al-Kubra*, 7:193 and his *Shu'ab al-Iman*, 6 (#2647) as well as al-Shawkani's *Nayl al-Awtar*, 1:93.

[15] See al-Marghinani's *al-Hidaya*, 4:461 and al-Babarti's commentary on *al-Hidaya* entitled *al-'Inaya Sharh al-Hidaya*,

قَالَ (وَيَنْظُرُ الرَّجُلُ مِنْ أَمَتِهِ الَّتِي تَحِلُّ لَهُ وَزَوْجَتِهِ إِلَى فَرْجِهَا) وَهَذَا إِطْلَاقٌ فِي النَّظَرِ إِلَى سَائِرِ بَدَنِهَا عَنْ شَهْوَةٍ وَغَيْرِ شَهْوَةٍ . وَالْأَصْلُ فِيهِ قَوْلُهُ عَلَيْهِ الصَّلَاةُ وَالسَّلَامُ " { غُضَّ بَصَرَكَ إِلَّا عَنْ أَمَتِكَ وَامْرَأَتِكَ } " وَلِأَنَّ مَا فَوْقَ ذَلِكَ مِنْ الْمَسِّ وَالْغَشَيَانِ مُبَاحٌ فَالنَّظَرُ أَوْلَى ، إِلَّا أَنَّ الْأَوْلَى أَنْ لَا يَنْظُرَ كُلُّ وَاحِدٍ مِنْهُمَا إِلَى عَوْرَةِ صَاحِبِهِ لِقَوْلِهِ عَلَيْهِ الصَّلَاةُ وَالسَّلَامُ " { إِذَا أَتَى أَحَدُكُمْ أَهْلَهُ فَلْيَسْتَتِرْ مَا اسْتَطَاعَ وَلَا يَتَجَرَّدَانِ تَجَرُّدَ الْعِيرِ } " وَلِأَنَّ ذَلِكَ يُورِثُ النِّسْيَانَ لِوُرُودِ الْأَثَرِ . وَكَانَ ابْنُ عُمَرَ رَضِيَ اللَّهُ عَنْهُمَا يَقُولُ : الْأَوْلَى أَنْ يَنْظُرَ لِيَكُونَ أَبْلَغَ فِي تَحْصِيلِ مَعْنَى اللَّذَّةِ (المرغناني، الهداية، ج 4 ص 461).

- In *al-Fatawa al-Hindiyya* it states:

14:241-242. This statement of Sayyiduna Ibn 'Umar (ra) is regarded as inauthentic according Imam Badr al-Din al-'Ayni as mentioned by Ibn 'Abidin in *Radd al-Muhtar*, 6:367:

"And Ibn 'Umar (ra) would say: 'it is better that one look [s: at the private parts of one's spouse] in order to attain the maximum pleasure.' However, as mentioned in al-'Ayni's commentary, there is neither an authentic nor a weak transmission channel (*isnad*) established for it from Ibn 'Umar…"

وكان ابن عمر رضي الله تعالى عنهما يقول الأولى أن ينظر ليكون أبلغ في تحصيل معنى اللذة اه لكن في شرحها للعيني أن هذا لم يثبت عن ابن عمر لا بسند صحيح ولا يسند ضعيف (ابن عابدين، رد المحتار ج 6 ص 367).

"[…] and there is no harm in both spouses being naked in their house as mentioned in [*Bughyat*] *al-Qunya* [of al-Qunawi]…"[16]

لَا بَأْسَ بِأَنْ يَتَجَرَّدَا فِي الْبَيْتِ كَذَا فِي الْقُنْيَةِ… (الفتاوى الهندية، ج 5 ص 328).

"[…] whatever is permitted to look at, it is also permitted to touch and his looking and feeling includes without a covering [s: or barrier]…"[17]

وما حَلَّ النَّظَرُ إِلَيْهِ حَلَّ مَسُّهُ وَنَظَرُهُ وَغَمْزُهُ من غَيْرِ حَائِلٍ… (الفتاوى الهندية، ج 5 ص 328).

- Imam al-Munawi (d. 1031/1621) explains the reason for the dislike (as mentioned in *al-Hidaya*) in gazing at one's spouse's *'awra* (nakedness) as follows:

"(**If anyone of you approaches his wife**) meaning for sex (**then let him cover himself**) meaning both covering themselves with a cloth which is recommended. He addressed [the men] to cover and not [the women] because he will be on top of her and if the top is covered it follows that the bottom is covered […] and this is out of modesty to Allah Most High and out of respect and etiquette to the Angels and guarding against shaytan's presence. If one does not cover up, then it is considered slightly disliked but not prohibitively disliked…"[18]

---

[16] See *al-Fatawa al-Hindiyya*, 5:328.
[17] See *al-Fatawa al-Hindiyya*, 5:328.
[18] Imam al-Munawi, *Fayd al-Qadir Sharh al-Jami' al-Saghir*, 1:307 (#340).

(إذا أتى أحدكم أهله) أي أراد جماع حليلته (فليستتر) أي فليتغط هو وإياها بثوب يسترهما ندبا وخاطبه بالستر دونها لأنه يعلوها وإذا استتر الأعلى استتر الأسفل (ولا يتجردان) خبر بمعنى النهي أي ينزعان الثياب عن عورتيهما فيصيران متجردين عما يسترهما (تجرد العيرين) تشبيه حذفت أداته وهو بفتح العين تثنية عير وهو الحمار الأهلي وغلب على الوحشي وذلك حياء من الله تعالى وأدبا مع الملائكة وحذرا من حضور الشيطان فإن فعل أحدهما ذلك كره تنزيها لا تحريما (المناوي، فيض القدير، جـ 1 ص 307 رقم 340).

- From the above evidences it is permitted therefore to be naked with one's spouse while in one's own dwelling although for reasons of etiquettes, it is better to cover with a sheet or blanket while engaged in sexual intercourse. From this, additional extended rulings include:

1. Spouses may be in a state of nudity within their home.

2. A husband may look at his wife's body lustfully and vice versa.

3. Spouses may watch each other in a state of nakedness.

4. Spouses may engage in full intercourse even without covering.

Foreplay acts:

[§3.1] Kissing (*taqbil* / التقبيل): Islam is emphatic on kissing as part of the sex experience and many *hadith* texts explicitly mention the permissibility of this:

"That the Prophet (saw) kissed one of his wives and then left for the prayer without performing *wudu'*. 'Urwa said: I asked ['A'isha]: It must have been you? ['A'isha] smiled."[19]

أن النبي صلى الله عليه وسلم قبل امرأة من نسائه ثم خرج إلى الصلاة ولم يتوضأ
قال عروة : فقلت لها : من هي إلا أنت فضحكت

"The Prophet (saw) would kiss ['A'isha] while he was fasting and he sucked on her tongue."[20]

---

[19] Narrated from 'A'isha by Abu Dawud (#179), Tirmidhi (#86) and Nasa'i (#170) each in their *Sunan* and al-Daraqutni in his *Sunan*, 1:49.

[20] Narrated from 'A'isha by Abu Dawud in his *Sunan* (#2386). See also, Diya' al-Maqdisi, *al-Sunan wa 'l-Ahkam*, 3:457; Ibn al-Qattan, *al-Wahm wa 'l-Iham*, 5:722; Ibn al-Qaysarani, *Dhakhirat al-Huffaz*, 2:814; Ibn 'Adi, *al-Kamil fi 'l-Du'afa'*, 3:176 and Ibn Taymiyya, *Sharh al-'Umda*, 1:484. The *hadith* can be read syntactically in two ways: either as two separate disjunctive sentences with two separate and different rulings or as one conjunctive sentence with the same ruling extending to both actions. Cf. al-'Azim Abadi, *'Awn al-Ma'bud*, p.1048. Thus, the readings would be:

Reading 1: The Prophet would kiss Umm al-Mu'minin 'A'isha (ra) **while** (= *waw al-hal*) in a state of fasting **and** (= *waw al-'atf*) suck on her tongue while in a state of fasting.

Reading 2: The Prophet would kiss Umm al-Mu'minin 'A'isha (ra) **while** (= *waw al-hal*) in a state of fasting **and** (= *waw al-'ibtida'i*) in another instance when he would not be fasting he would suck on her tongue.

أن النبي صلى الله عليه وسلم كان يقبلها وهو صائم ويمص لسانها...

- Imam al-Munawi in his commentary *Fayd al-Qadir* states that it is an emphasized *sunna* of the Prophet (saw) to be engaged in foreplay:

كان إذا اجتلى النساء أقعى و قبل...

"When a man undresses the woman, he should sit beside her and kiss her" [...] **(and kiss)** the woman who he sits next to desiring sex with her and it is taken as a *sunna mu'akkada* (emphasized *sunna*) to engage in foreplay, kissing and sucking on the tongue before sexual intercourse and it is disliked to do otherwise [...]."[21]

(وقبل) المرأة التي قعد لها يريد جماعها وأخذوا منه أنه يسن مؤكدا تقديم المداعبة والتقبيل ومص اللسان على الجماع وكرهوا خلافه (المناوي، فيض القدير جـ 5 ص 115 رقم : 6536).

- Kissing one's spouse is a *sunna* of the beloved Messenger of Allah – especially in leaving and returning to one's wife say from work or leaving the house to go to the Mosque or returning from *dawah* purposes, etc.

- From the above narration the following rulings are permitted:

1. One may kiss, suck, lick and moisten his partner's lips.

---

[21] See al-Munawi, *Fayd al-Qadir Sharh al-Jami' al-Saghir*, 5:115 (#6536).

2. Couples may passionately kiss.

3. Couples may suck each other's tongue.

4. Couples may lick each other's tongue.

- Spouses may kiss each other all over their bodies including genitals, hands, arms, shoulders, back, buttocks, stomach, thighs, legs and feet.

[§3.2] **Caressing** (*mass* / المس): there is general permissibility for spouses to stroke lightly and in a loving and endearing manner any part of the body, including genitals, hands, arms, shoulders, back, buttocks, stomach, thighs, legs and feet.

- Affection and longing should underpin the intimacy of both partners and each should seek the pleasure of the other:

"Indeed, if a man looks at his wife [out of love and affection] and she looks at him, Allah looks at them both with Mercy. When he holds her hands [out of love and affection], their sins fall from the gaps between their fingers."[22]

إن الرجل إذا نظر إلى امرأته و نظرت إليه نظر الله إليهما نظرة رحمة، فإذا أخذ بكفها، تساقطت ذنوبهما من خلال أصابعهما...

---

[22] Narrated from Abu Sa'id al-Khudri by al-Muttaqi al-Hindi in *Kanz al-'Ummal* (#44437). The narration has weakness in it due to the transmitter Isma'il b. Yahya al-Taymi who is a known forger of *hadith*. Cf. al-Albani, *Silsilat Ahadith al-Da'ifa*, (#3274) and *Da'if al-Jami'* (#1447).

- Any permitted means (*wasa'il*) that will enable the spouses to achieve intimacy and pleasure will also be permitted. This may include for example exploring each other's erogenous zones or bodily sensual locations.

[§3.3] Rubbing (*dalk* / الدلك): Our sacred Shari'a permits spouses to completely enjoy each other and to mutually derive pleasure from each other. This means every part unless specifically prohibited.

- In the school of Imam Abu Hanifa, there are little or no restrictions in the way of foreplay and amorous prelude. In fact, it is considered, as Imam al-Munawi mentioned, an emphasized *sunna* emulating the beautiful conduct of the Messenger of Allah (saw).

- It is permitted for the wife to stroke, cup, and hold and affectionately play with her husband's penis.

- It is also permitted for the wife to fully masturbate (*al-istimna'*) her husband and make him ejaculate by using:

1. Her breasts.
2. Her thighs.
3. Her hands.
4. Her feet.
5. Her stomach.
6. Her buttocks.

"[…] and his saying (**it is disliked** [s: here referring to the act of the wife masturbating her husband until he ejaculates from the *fiqh* work *al-Jawharat al-Nayyira*]) in its apparent sense means slightly disliked (*karaha tanzih*) because it is the same as a man ejaculating through his wife rubbing him with her thighs (*takhfidh*) or her stomach (*tabtin*)…"[23]

(قَوْلُهُ كُرِهَ) الظَّاهِرُ أَنَّهَا كَرَاهَةُ تَنْزِيهٍ ؛ لِأَنَّ ذَلِكَ بِمَنْزِلَةِ مَا لَوْ أَنْزَلَ بِتَفْخِيذٍ أَوْ تَبْطِينٍ تَأَمَّلْ وَقَدَّمْنَا عَنْ الْمِعْرَاجِ فِي بَابِ مُفْسِدَاتِ الصَّوْمِ (ابن عابدين، رد المحتار جـ 4 ص 27).

- In *al-Fatawa al-Hindiyya* and *Radd al-Muhtar* it states respectively:

"It is not permitted to masturbate [one's self] and there is a penalty in it (*wa fihi ta'zir*). However, if one's wife or servant-girl playfully strokes his penis and he ejaculates, then it is considered disliked and nothing will happen to him [s: in terms of legal penalty or punishment]."[24]

الِاسْتِمْنَاءُ حَرَامٌ وَفِيهِ التَّعْزِيرُ وَلَوْ مَكَّنَ امْرَأَتَهُ أَوْ أَمَتَهُ مِنَ الْعَبَثِ بِذَكَرِهِ فَأَنْزَلَ فإنه مَكْرُوهٌ وَلَا شَيْءَ عليه (الفتاوى الهندية، جـ 2 ص 170).

"It is permitted for a man to be masturbated by his wife or servant-girl. Refer to what we have discussed there. His stating (**nothing will happen to him**) means no *hadd* penalty or discretionary penalty will

---

[23] Ibn 'Abidin, *Radd al-Muhtar*, 4:27. It is also considered disliked because semen is wasted.
[24] Ibn 'Abidin, *Radd al-Muhtar*, 4:27. Refer to *al-Fatawa al-Hindiyya*, 2:170 for the quote.

be administered..."[25]

يَجُوزُ أَنْ يَسْتَمْنِيَ بِيَدِ زَوْجَتِهِ أَوْ خَادِمَتِهِ ، وَانْظُرْ مَا كَتَبْنَاهُ هُنَاكَ (قَوْلُهُ وَلَا شَيْءَ عَلَيْهِ) أَيْ مِنْ حَدٍّ وَتَعْزِيرٍ... (ابن عابدين، رد المحتار ج 4 ص 27).

- The same general permissibility of the above holds for the husband with regards to his wife. He may for example:

    1. Fondle, kiss, caress, suck and lick his wife's breast.

    2. Fondle, kiss, caress, suck and lick his wife's pudendum.

    3. Fully masturbate her until she reaches orgasm.

- Again, in *al-Fatawa al-Hindiyya* it has the clear statement of Imam Abu Hanifa:

"Abu Yusuf – Allah Most High have mercy on him – I asked Abu Hanifa – Allah Most High have mercy on him – about a man who touches the vagina of his wife and she touches his penis in order to give him an erection; do you see anything wrong with that? He replied: No. In fact, I hope they will get reward for it. This was mentioned in *al-Khulasa*."[26]

قال أَبُو يُوسُفَ رَحِمَهُ اللَّهُ تَعَالَى سَأَلْتُ أَبَا حَنِيفَةَ رَحِمَهُ اللَّهُ تَعَالَى عن رَجُلٍ يَمَسُّ فَرْجَ امْرَأَتِهِ وَهِيَ تَمَسُّ فَرْجَهُ لِتُحَرِّكَ آلَتَهُ هل تَرَى بِذَلِكَ بَأْسًا قال لَا وَأَرْجُو أَنْ

---

[25] Ibn 'Abidin, *Radd al-Muhtar*, 4:27.
[26] See *al-Fatawa al-Hindiyya*, 5:328.

يُعْطَى الْأَجْرَ كَذَا في الْخُلَاصَةِ (الفتاوى الهندية، ج 5 ص 328).

[§3.4] Beautification (*al-tazayyun* / التزين):
There is nothing in Islam that hinders men and women from being clean, presentable and adorned.

- It is against Islamic grooming provisions to look unattractive, dirty, and unsightly and there are numerous *ahadith* in this regard. Unfortunately, Muslims fall very short of this.

- The more specific focus of this sub-section is the permissibility of beautification and seduction amongst couples as a means of foreplay.

- Given what has been mentioned and discussed above, the following rulings are permitted for the wife **only for her husband**:

    1. To be naked for her husband.

    2. To wear sexy lingerie for her husband.

    3. To wear full make-up for her husband (which includes adorning herself with gold and silver jewelry).

    4. To wax and shave for her husband (including full wax).

    5. To dress-up beautifully for her husband (e.g. in sarees, dresses, etc.).

- It is very thoughtful of the wife to do her utmost to please her husband and our Sacred Law has given women exceptions so as to achieve this; for example the removal of facial hair (*izalat sha'r al-wajh*) if it becomes unsightly:

"...and in *Tabyin al-Maharim* it has that removing hair from the face is not permitted except if a women appears to sprout a beard or moustache which in that case she may remove it. In fact it would be recommended to do so..."[27]

وفي تبيين المحارم إزالة الشعر من الوجه حرام إلا إذا نبت للمرأة لحية أو شوارب فلا تحرم إزالته بل تستحب (ابن عابدين، رد المحتار ج 6 ص 373).

- Another exception is the dispensation not to wash the full hair for a purification bath (*ghusl*) after sex. One of the known obligatory aspects (*fard*) of the *ghusl* is washing the hair completely and hence must be performed. However, to make matters easy, if extended marital relations are fulfilled at night, then one ritual bath (*ghusl*) would suffice for each instance. In the Hanafi School, a woman is granted latitude in this particular case. She is permitted to merely wipe her head instead of the full wash if she fears falling ill or fears increasing her suffering, exacerbating and escalating her illness and as a result withholds herself from her husband. Imam Ibn 'Abidin states the following:

"Regarding his statement: قوله (ولا تمنع نفسها) أي خوفا **(and does not withhold**

---

[27] Ibn 'Abidin, *Radd al-Muhtar*, 6:373.

herself) meaning out of fear of the obligatory aspects of the *ghusl* she has to fulfill if he [desires] sex with her because of his right to do so. In this she has the choice of not washing her hair..."²⁸

من وجوب الغسل عليها إذا وطهئا لأنه حقه ولها مندوحة عن غسل رأسها...

- Any means that assists and strengthens the desire and attraction between spouses should be pursued e.g. exercise and keeping fit unless there is a specific *shar'i* prohibition. How sad it is to see Muslim men, women and couples today give little or no attention to exercise or keeping fit through a healthy life-style. How it would increase the physical attraction and mutual desire if each spouse were physically fit and in shape so as to maintain the marriage in and out of the bedroom! If the intention is this then Allah will surely reward each of them for it.

- It must further be emphasized that although the wife is highly encouraged to beautify and present herself to her husband for his pleasure, Islam requires the husband to also meet his wife's desires and needs.

- All too often Muslim husbands make demands (often excessive) on their wives to look and appear attractive but insist that their wives ought to have no expectations on them. This is clearly against Islamic teachings.

---

[28] See Ibn 'Abidin, *Radd al-Muhtar*, 1:153.

- Muslim men should heed the wonderful statement of Sayyiduna Ibn 'Abbas (ra):

"Ibn 'Abbas (ra) used to say: 'Indeed, I love to adorn myself for my wife as much as I love her to adorn herself for me'…"[29]

و قد كان ابن عباس رضي الله عنهما يقول : إني لأحب أن أتزين للمرأة كما أحب أن تتزين لي (ابن الجوزي، صيد الخاطر ص **142**).

- The Holy Prophet (saw) is reported to have said:

"Wash your clothes, take care of your hair, use the *siwak*, adorn yourself and keep clean for Banu Isra'il did not used to do that and so their women committed adultery…"[30]

اغسلوا ثيابكم، و خذوا من شعوركم، و استاكوا، و تزينوا، و تنظفوا، فإن بني إسرائيل لم يكونوا يفعلون ذلك، فزنت نساؤهم

- Muslim men must make correct preparations such as the following:

---

[29] As mentioned by Imam Ibn al-Jawzi in his semi-autobiographical musing, *Sayd al-Khatir*, p.142.
[30] See al-Hindi, *Kanz al-'Ummal* (#17175) and Ibn 'Asakir in his *Ta'rikh Dimashq*, 36:124. The narration is weak due to the transmitter 'Abd Allah ibn Maymun al-Qaddah whose narrations are rejected as mentioned by al-Hafiz Ibn Hajar al-'Asqalani and al-Dhahabi in *Tadhkirat al-Huffaz*, 3:1158. See for example al-Albani, *Da'if al-Jami'* (#987) and his *Silislat Ahadith al-Da'ifa* (#7029).

1. **Hygiene and cleanliness**: Men should:

[1] grooming their hair and beard so as to appear smart and well-presented,[31]

[2] wearing perfumes in order to smell nice,[32]

[3] removing any odour and bad smells from the body and mouth (e.g. tobacco smells, shisha smells, sweat, etc.);[33]

[4] ensuring private parts are kept shaved, washed, clean and free of bad smell[34] and

[5] wearing washed, clean, tidy and ironed clothes.[35]

2. **Health and Fitness**: Men should: [1] attempt to eat healthily and [2] exercise regularly in order to remain fit and physically attractive.

- Imam Ibn al-Jawzi (d. 597/1200) beautifully remarks about a husband who keeps himself attractive for his wife:

"Then, he will become likeable to his wife in this condition [s: of being attractive and well-groomed]. For indeed, women are the other half (*shaqa'iq*; lit. = 'sister') of men. Just as he may dislike something in her, likewise she may dislike something in him. It may be that he endures and has patience over something that he dislikes in her but she does not [s: have patience over something *she* dislikes of him]. I

---

[31] See Abu Dawud, *Sunan* (#4160).
[32] See Muslim, *Sahih* (#2252).
[33] See Muslim, *Sahih* (#255).
[34] See Tirmidhi, *Sunan* (#19).
[35] See Abu Dawud, *Sunan* (#4059) and Ahmad, *Musnad*, 4/180.

have seen a group of people who claim to be *zuhhad* [s: those who live an austere life, doing without] but yet they are the most dirty and unclean people. This is because their knowledge did not set them right."[36]

ثم إنه يؤنس الزوجة بتلك الحال . فإن النساء شقائق الرجال، فكما أنه يكره الشيء منها، فكذلك هي تكرهه، ربما صبر هو على ما يكره و هي لا تصبر. و قد رأيت جماعة يزعمون أنهم زهاد . و هم من أقذر الناس، و ذلك أنهم ما قومهم العلم (ابن الجوزي، صيد الخاطر ص **142**).

- Men must realize that they can be very unattractive to their wives and only out of humility, shyness and consideration for their husbands' feelings, do not directly mention it. May Allah reward our sisters for their perseverance! *Amin*.

[§3.5] Fantasising (*tasawwur* / التصور): there is no prohibition on spouses to fantasise about each other **as long as it is restricted to themselves only**.

- Whatever is permitted to actually perform, it follows by analogy it is permitted to think about.

- However, it is explicitly forbidden to fantasise – whether in foreplay or during sex – about another woman/man or women/men other than one's wife (*ajnabiyya*) or husband. This is considered a category of *zina*

---

[36] Ibn al-Jawzi, *Sayd al-Khatir*, pp.142-143.

('fornication').[37] Imam Ibn 'Abidin presents the discussion as follows:

"Ibn al-Haj al-Maliki said that it is prohibited [s: to think of another woman while having sex with one's wife] because it is a form of fornication (*zina*). And our scholars have said regarding one who takes a glass [of water] and drinks from it imagining it to be wine then [at that moment] the water becomes unlawful for him [...] The

---

[37] The word "*zina*" (زنى) can mean more than just extra-marital sex or fornication. It can involve other parts of the body which are utilized for ill intentions and perverse sexual aims. Thus, it takes a more generic meaning. A *hadith* from Abu Hurayra (ra) related from the Prophet (saw) states that:

"**Allah has decreed for every son of Adam his share of *zina*, and there is no way to escape from it. The *zina* of the eye is a glance, the *zina* of the tongue is speaking and the *zina* of the mind is wishing and desiring; then the private part either acts upon this or it does not...**" See Bukhari (#6243) and Muslim (#2657) in their *Sahihs*.

إِنَّ اللَّهَ كَتَبَ عَلَى ابْنِ آدَمَ حَظَّهُ مِنْ الزِّنَا أَدْرَكَ ذَلِكَ لَا مَحَالَةَ، فَزِنَا الْعَيْنِ النَّظَرُ، وَزِنَا اللِّسَانِ الْمَنْطِقُ، وَالنَّفْسُ تَمَنَّى وَتَشْتَهِي، وَالْفَرْجُ يُصَدِّقُ ذَلِكَ كُلَّهُ وَيُكَذِّبُهُ

Ibn Hajar comments: "...and *zina* is not restricted to the private parts; rather it can include other than the private parts such the gaze and the like..." Ibn Battal explains the *hadith* cited above to mean: "Looking and speaking are described as '*zina*' because they actually lead to *zina*. This is why he [s: the Prophet] said that the private part either acts upon this or it does not..." Ibn Hajar, *Fath al-Bari* 12:28:

الزنا لا يختص إطلاقه بالفرج بل يطلق على ما دون الفرج من نظر وغيره...

سُمِّيَ النَّظَرُ وَالنُّطْقُ زِنًا لِأَنَّهُ يَدْعُو إِلَى الزِّنَا الْحَقِيقِيِّ. وَلِذَلِكَ قَالَ (وَالْفَرْجُ يُصَدِّق ذَلِكَ وَيُكَذِّبُهُ)

strongest opinion in our School is that it is not permitted because to imagine having sex with a woman who is a stranger is to imagine actually and directly committing a sin and so it becomes similar to the example of drinking water [s: thinking it is wine]. I then saw the author of *Tabyin al-Maharim* – one of our scholars – transmit the words of Ibn al-Haj al-Maliki affirming it where at the end his words were, 'if a person drinks water thinking it to be an intoxicant, that [water] becomes unlawful for him.'..."[38]

وقال ابن الحاج المالكي إنه يحرم لأنه نوع من الزنا كما قال علماؤنا فيمن أخذ كوزا يشرب منه فتصور بين عينيه أنه خمر فشربه أن ذلك الماء يصير حراما عليه ...

والأقرب لقواعد مذهبنا عدم الحل لأن تصور تلك الأجنبية بين يديه يطؤها فيه تصوير مباشرة المعصية على هيئتها فهو نظير مسألة الشرب ثم رأيت صاحب تبيين المحارم من علمائنا نقل عبارة ابن الحاج المالكي وأقرها وفي آخرها حديث عنه إذا شرب العبد الماء على شبه المسكر كان ذلك عليه حراما...(ابن عابدين، رد المحتار جـ 6 ص 372).

- From this, extended and other general prohibitions would include:

1. Fantasising about one's second wife while having sex with the first.

---

[38] Ibn 'Abidin, *Radd al-Muhtar*, 6:372.

2. Insisting that one's wife act, dress up or play the role of another woman (e.g. a specific actress, singer, dancer, etc.).

3. Insisting on one's wife to wear clothes prohibited in Islam due to ideological or religious connotations (e.g. nun's dress, communist clothing, etc.) and vice-versa.

[§3.6] Sex Toys: also known as adult toys or marital aids, these are objects or devices employed to facilitate human sexual pleasure or to stimulate sexual parts for enhancement and arousal.

- Despite the immediate show of disgust and condemnation of these toys by some ultra-traditionally minded scholars, it is not strictly speaking unlawful. However, the disgust and proclamation expressed in *fatwas* against using such toys are motivated by pious intentions especially in how these toys, gadgets and instruments are evidently linked to or associated with the adult entertainment industry. Nevertheless, there are grounds for the permissibility of employing adult toys for additional sexual stimulation.

- One *fatwa* on this particular *mas'ala* (legal issue) reads:

Regarding the use of Sex toys, their use is permissible with the following conditions: 1. It should not cause any internal or external-harm to the body 2. It should not contain any haraam ingredients, 3. It should not be inserted into the inner-private part of the women; rather such toys should be used that stimulate the outer private parts, such as the clitoris. 4. It should only be used in foreplay and in order to enhance the act of intercourse, not to substitute it. 5. It should not be used so often that it becomes an integral part of the intercourse, so much so that the spouse then cannot gain sexual gratification without it. 6. One should also ensure that he does not commit any Haraam act when acquiring these toys nor should he go to any places of Haraam, such as adult gift shops. Even though one will be going for a valid reason, he is sure to look at Haraam pictures and others who see him enter will probably entertain evil thoughts about him (Fatwa #10326).[39]

- Another *fatwa* regarding sex aids/toys reads:

  Using an aid such as a vibrator to stimulate any part of the body except the private parts, or to stimulate the outer private parts of the wife, including her clitoris, is also permitted. The proviso is that it must be used by one's spouse and not by the person themselves. To use such aids alone as a means of alleviating one's loneliness is sinful and would be considered a form of masturbation.[40]

- Based on the above, there is an evident caution here which is that any fear, likelihood or probability that using these toys will lead the spouses to committing impermissible acts, they should at that point avoided it altogether.

- Other general and extended rulings permitted for both spouses within this section include:

1. The wife assuming erotic postures and positions to arouse her husband.

---

[39] See Mufti Ebrahim Desai http://www.askimam.org
[40] Muhammad ibn Adam al-Kawthari, *Islamic Guide to Sexual Relations*, p.68.

2. The wife behaving in an enticing and erotic way to arouse her husband.

3. Each partner slowly undressing the other.

4. Each partner rubbing their private parts with their clothes on.

5. Each partner touching and massaging erogenous zones with their clothes on.

6. Each partner whispering provocative and erotic language into the others ear.

7. Smacking wife's bottom playfully during foreplay and vice versa.

8. Erotic massage with permitted lubricants and oils.

- From the outlines given above, we can present the basic rulings within this section as follows:

[1] Permitted (*mubah*)

- For both spouses to kiss, caress, lick, suck, fondle and stroke each other all over their body parts.

- For the wife to unrestrictedly beautify herself for her husband.

- For both spouses to masturbate and stimulate each other.

- **Conditionally** permitted for a wife to dance for her husband.[41]

- **Conditionally** permitted to use sex toys.

- For the wife to sexually tease and entice her husband.

[2] Disliked (*makruh*)

- To excessively masturbate the husband until ejaculation.

- To indulge excessively with the use of sex toys.

- Spanking, slapping and rough sex.

[3] Prohibited (*haram*)

- To insert sexual toys into any private part.

- To self-stimulate by masturbating with one's own hands or any sexual toy/accessory.

- To actually role-play.

- To engage in extreme foreplay, fetishes and deprivation acts, etc.

- To fantasise about another woman during sex or foreplay

---

[41] See H. A. al-Tahir, *Tuhfat al-'Arus*, p.185.

§4. Oral Sex

———— ♦ ————

- Oral sex is a mode of sexual contact well-known in western popular cultural references.

- Oral sex has is depicted as a normalized part of marriages or relationships in the West and classical Muslim scholars have also delineated views regarding it.

- Oral sex is the stimulation of a spouse's genitalia through the organ of the mouth. Stimulation of female genitalia with the mouth is termed *cunnilingus* and stimulation of male genitalia is termed *fellatio* or *irrumatio*.

- In sexual activity, oral sex usually constitutes part of the foreplay within the sequence of sex but it can also be engaged in post-sex acts as after-play.

- The noble jurists of the Hanafi School have mixed views regarding oral sex where the husband kisses, licks or sucks his wife's vagina or where the wife takes the husband's penis into her mouth and orally stimulates him. The major motivation is the high risk of swallowing pre-ejaculatory fluid (*madhy*) and semen (*many*) or the woman's pre-sexual discharge because all are considered impure (*najis*) by the Hanafi School. The reasoning is much like this as follows:

P1. Any genital discharge is impure.
P2. It is not permissible to take impure substances into the mouth.
P3. Oral sex involves an extremely high possibility of swallowing or taking impure substances directly into the mouth.

Therefore,
C. It is prohibitively disliked to engage in oral sex.

- On this view above, it would **not** be permitted:

1. For the wife to lick or suck the penis in order to arouse or stimulate.
2. For the husband to lick, suck or insert his tongue into his wife's vagina in order to arouse or induce clitoral stimulation.

- In *al-Fatawa al-Hindiyya* it states:

"In *al-Nawazil* it has: if a man inserts his penis in the mouth of his wife then it is said by some, to be disliked…"[42]

في النوازل إذا أدخل الرجل ذكره في فم امرأته قد قيل يكره (الفتاوى الهندية، ج 5 ص 372).

---

[42] See *al-Fatawa al-Hindiyya*, 5:372.

- In *al-Muhit al-Burhani* of Imam Mahmud b. Ahmad al-Bukhari (d. 1219) it has the following:

"If a man inserts his penis into his wife's mouth, it is said by some that this is disliked because [the mouth] is the place from which the Qur'an is recited and would thus not be fitting for the penis to be inserted into it. <u>Others have said otherwise…</u>"[43]

إذا أدخل الرجل ذكره فم أمرأته فقد قيل: يكره؛ لأنه موضع قراءة القرآن، فلا يليق به إدخال الذكر فيه، <u>وقد قيل بخلافه</u> (البخاري المحيط البرهاني، جـ 8 ص 132).

- According to the position that deems oral sex permitted, it would be additionally permitted:

1. For the wife to merely kiss or lick the penis.
2. For the husband to merely kiss or lick the pudendum.

- Therefore, there is a noted difference amongst Hanafi *fuqaha'* over the act of inserting the penis into the mouth and we can tabularize the basic rulings within this section as follows:

Permitted (*mubah*)	**Extremely disliked** (*makruh tahrimi*)
- As long as no sexual fluids enters the mouth and is swallowed.	- Because of the likelihood of sexual fluids entering the mouth and it being

---

[43] al-Bukhari, *al-Muhit al-Burhani*, 8:134.

swallowed.

- Because it is the organ of devotion to Allah.

- Because it contravenes religious propriety.

- Because it contravenes overall Islamic endeavour of inculcating modesty and shame (*haya'*).

- The cautionary view of the Hanafi School is that full oral sex ought to be avoided.[44]

---

[44] For a discussion, see al-Tahir, *Tuhfat al-'Arus*, pp.200-202 and al-Jibaly, *Closer than a Garment*, pp.22-24.

§5. Sexual Intercourse

──◆──

- Islam is a sex positive faith.

- It neither stigmatizes sex nor does it outlaw it.

- Islam recognizes that human beings have an instinct to procreate, i.e. an innate constituted dimension to their nature that prompts sexual desire that requires gratification and indeed allows this desire to be satiated.

- Although the physical engagement of sex is an important and required dimension of a marriage, Islam has not even left this intimate act un-regulated.

- There are some basic preliminaries to the actual sex act that ought to be heeded as discussed in the books of *fiqh*:

[§5.1] Definition of 'intercourse':

- From general indications of the *hadith* texts, 'sexual intercourse' is considered to have occurred when the head of the penis (*hashafa / ra's al-dhakar*) enters the vagina, i.e. when the tip fully disappears into the vagina. The *hadith* this definition is derived from reads as follows: "**When a man sits (*jalasa*) between the four parts [s: of his wife such as her arms, legs, thighs, etc.] and then has intercourse with her (*jahadaha*), the *ghusl* (bath) becomes mandatory for him...**"[45]

---

[45] Bukhari (#291) and Muslim (#525) in their *Sahihs*.

اذَا جَلَسَ بَيْنَ شُعَبِهَا الْأَرْبَعِ ثُمَّ جَهَدَهَا فَقَدْ وَجَبَ عَلَيْهِ الْغُسْلُ

- The verb <جَلَسَ> – literally meaning 'to sit' – but in the *hadith* means 'sex' and the verb <جَهَدَهَا> in the *hadith* means 'penetration'. Both are non-literal (metonymic) expressions.[46]

- Another *hadith* of the Prophet presents the following expression: "**…when the two circumcised parts touch…**"[47]

---

[46] Ibn Hajar, *Fath al-Bari*, 2:470-471:

وَهُوَ كِنَايَةٌ عَنْ الْجِمَاعِ...

وَهَذَا يَدُلُّ عَلَى أَنَّ الْجَهْدَ هُنَا كِنَايَةٌ عَنْ مُعَالَجَةِ الْإِيلَاجِ وَرَوَاهُ الْبَيْهَقِيّ مِنْ طَرِيقِ ابْنِ أَبِي عَرُوبَةَ عَنْ قَتَادَةَ مُخْتَصَرًا وَلَفْظُهُ " إِذَا الْتَقَى الْخِتَانَانِ فَقَدْ وَجَبَ الْغُسْلُ " وَهَذَا مُطَابِقٌ لِلَفْظِ التَّرْجَمَةِ فَكَأَنَّ الْمُصَنِّفَ أَشَارَ إِلَى هَذِهِ الرِّوَايَةِ كَعَادَتِهِ فِي التَّبْوِيبِ بِلَفْظِ إِحْدَى رِوَايَاتِ حَدِيثِ الْبَابِ (ابن حجر، فتح الباري جـ 2 ص 470)

[47] Muslim, *Sahih* (#349). Ibn Hajar, *Fath al-Bari*, :

الْمُرَادُ بِالْمَسِّ وَالِالْتِقَاءِ الْمُحَاذَاةُ وَيَدُلُّ عَلَيْهِ رِوَايَةُ التِّرْمِذِيِّ بِلَفْظِ " إِذَا جَاوَزَ " وَلَيْسَ الْمُرَادُ بِالْمَسِّ حَقِيقَتَهُ؛ لِأَنَّهُ لَا يُتَصَوَّرُ عِنْدَ غَيْبَةِ الْحَشَفَةِ وَلَوْ حَصَلَ الْمَسُّ قَبْلَ الْإِيلَاجِ لَمْ يَجِبْ الْغُسْلُ بِالْإِجْمَاعِ قَالَ النَّوَوِيّ: مَعْنَى الْحَدِيثِ أَنَّ إِيجَابَ الْغُسْلِ لَا يَتَوَقَّفُ عَلَى الْإِنْزَالِ وَتُعُقِّبَ بِأَنَّهُ يُحْتَمَلُ أَنْ يُرَادَ بِالْجَهْدِ الْإِنْزَالُ؛ لِأَنَّهُ هُوَ الْغَايَةُ فِي الْأَمْرِ فَلَا يَكُونُ فِيهِ دَلِيلٌ وَالْجَوَابُ أَنَّ التَّصْرِيحَ بِعَدَمِ التَّوَقُّفِ عَلَى الْإِنْزَالِ قَدْ وَرَدَ فِي بَعْضِ طُرُقِ الْحَدِيثِ الْمَذْكُورِ فَانْتَفَى الِاحْتِمَالُ فَفِي رِوَايَةِ مُسْلِمٍ مِنْ طَرِيقِ مَطَرٍ الْوَرَّاقِ عَنْ الْحَسَنِ فِي آخِرِ هَذَا الْحَدِيثِ " وَإِنْ لَمْ يُنْزِلْ " وَوَقَعَ ذَلِكَ فِي رِوَايَةِ قَتَادَةَ أَيْضًا رَوَاهُ ابْنُ أَبِي خَيْثَمَةَ فِي تَارِيخِهِ عَنْ عَفَّانَ قَالَ حَدَّثَنَا هَمَّامٌ وَأَبَانُ قَالَا حَدَّثَنَا قَتَادَةُ بِهِ وَزَادَ فِي آخِرِهِ " أَنْزَلَ أَوْ لَمْ يُنْزِلْ " وَكَذَا رَوَاهُ الدَّارَقُطْنِيّ وَصَحَّحَهُ مِنْ طَرِيقِ عَلِيّ بْنِ سَهْلٍ عَنْ عَفَّانَ، وَكَذَا ذَكَرَهَا أَبُو دَاوُد الطَّيَالِسِيّ عَنْ حَمَّادِ بْنِ سَلَمَةَ عَنْ قَتَادَةَ (ابن حجر، فتح الباري جـ 2 ص 471)

إِذَا جَلَسَ بَيْنَ شُعَبِهَا الْأَرْبَعِ وَمَسَّ الْخِتَانُ الْخِتَانَ فَقَدْ وَجَبَ الْغُسْلُ

- Imam al-Nawawi explains the meaning of the *hadiths* in a little more detail as follows:

"With regard to his (saw) phrase: **"when the two circumcised part touch, then *ghusl* is obligatory"**, the scholars have said: what this means is when your penis disappears into her vagina; it does not mean touching in the real or literal sense. That is because the circumcised part of a woman is above the vagina and the penis does not touch it during intercourse. The scholars are unanimously agreed that if he places his penis on the circumcised part and does not penetrate her, then no *ghusl* is required, neither for him nor for her. The fact that what is meant is what we have mentioned and that what is meant by both touching (*al-mumasa*) is the two parts coming in line with one another is indicated by another narration that reads: **"when the two circumcised parts meet"** i.e., coming in line with one another…"[48]

قَوْله صَلَّى اللَّه عَلَيْهِ وَسَلَّمَ : (وَمَسَّ الْخِتَانُ الْخِتَانَ فَقَدْ وَجَبَ الْغُسْل) قَالَ الْعُلَمَاء: مَعْنَاهُ غَيَّبْت ذَكَرك فِي فَرْجهَا، وَلَيْسَ الْمُرَاد حَقِيقَة الْمَسّ، وَذَلِكَ أَنَّ خِتَان الْمَرْأَة فِي أَعْلَى الْفَرْج، وَلَا يَمَسّهُ الذَّكَر فِي الْجِمَاع، وَقَدْ أَجْمَعَ الْعُلَمَاء عَلَى أَنَّهُ لَوْ وَضَعَ ذَكَرُهُ عَلَى خِتَانهَا وَلَمْ يُولِجْهُ (يُدخله) لَمْ يَجِب الْغُسْل لَا عَلَيْهِ، وَلَا عَلَيْهَا، فَدَلَّ عَلَى أَنَّ الْمُرَاد مَا ذَكَرْنَاهُ. وَالْمُرَاد بِالْمُمَاسَّةِ: الْمُحَاذَاة، وَكَذَلِكَ الرِّوَايَة الْأُخْرَى: (إِذَا اِلْتَقَى الْخِتَانَانِ) أَيْ : تَحَاذَيَا (النووي، شرح صحيح مسلم رقم حديث 349)

- al-Nawawi then states in his expanded legal commentary *al-Majmu'*:

---

[48] al-Nawawi, *Sharh Sahih Muslim* (#349).

"The obligation of *ghusl* and all other rulings that are connected to intercourse are subject to the condition that the tip of the penis disappears completely into the vagina and they are not dependent on more than that. None of the rulings have to with part of the tip disappearing only..."[49]

وجوب الغسل وجميع الأحكام المتعلقة بالجماع يشترط فيها تغييب الحشفة بكمالها في الفرج، ولا يشترط زيادة (على) الحشفة، ولا يتعلق ببعض الحشفة وحده شيء من الأحكام (النووي، المجموع جـ 2 ص 150)

- Imam Ibn Hajar remarks:

"What is meant by 'touching' (*mass*) and 'meeting' (*iltiqa'*) is coming in line with one another (*muhadhat*), which is indicated by a report narrated by al-Tirmidhi with the wording: **"when it goes beyond [s: i.e. penetrates]"**. It does not mean touching in a literal sense, because that does not happen when the tip of the penis disappears..."[50]

وَالْمُرَاد بِالْمَسِّ وَالِالْتِقَاءِ: الْمُحَاذَاة، وَيَدُلُّ عَلَيْهِ رِوَايَة التِّرْمِذِيّ بِلَفْظ: (إِذَا جَاوَزَ) وَلَيْسَ الْمُرَاد بِالْمَسِّ حَقِيقَته، لِأَنَّهُ لَا يُتَصَوَّرُ عِنْدَ غَيْبَة الْحَشَفَة

[§5.2] Privacy (*khalwa* / الخلوى): couples desiring to have sex must be in total seclusion (*khalwa*). This means there should be no-one able to witness the act itself. All means of achieving this must be exhausted, e.g.

1. Locking the door.
2. Shutting windows.

---

[49] *al-Majmu' Sharh al-Muhadhdhab*, 2:150.
[50] Ibn Hajar, *Fath al-Bari*, 2:471.

3. Pulling the blinds.
4. Ensuring no child is in the room.
5. Etc.

- Privacy also entails that while in the sexual act, couples minimize noise as much as possible as it is against Islamic stipulations of modesty to enable others to know this is taking place. This is especially the case if others are at home such as in-laws, parents or elder children.

- In *Radd al-Muhtar* of Imam Ibn 'Abidin (d. 1836) it states:

"It is [prohibitively] disliked for a man to make love to his wife in the presence of discerning children, blind people, a second wife, either of their servant girls…"[51]

ويكره للرجل أن يطأ امرأته وعندها صبي يعقل أو أعمى أو ضرتها أو أمتها أو أمته (ابن عابدين، رد المحتار جـ 3 ص 208).

- The fact that it is prohibited to perform sex in front of a blind person is because h/she is still able to hear it.

- If it is the case that couples are unable to perform sex without it being evident, then they should restrain and withhold until a more appropriate time.

- From the above, the following are **explicitly prohibited**:

---

[51] Ibn 'Abidin, *Radd al-Muhtar*, 3:208.

1. Performing sex or engaging in any sexual conduct in public areas (parks, shops, public toilets, street corners, beaches, cars, etc.): based on the impermissibility of actually having sex in a non-enclosed and non-private place (e.g. hotel room, bedroom, etc.).

2. Performing sex to an audience (e.g. through web-cam, etc.): based on the impermissibility of talking about sex to others where by analogy it is worse to actually show the contents.

3. Performing sex in front of the husband's second wife: based on the impermissibility of looking at the *'awra* of another and contravening the requirement for sex to be non-intrusive and private.[52]

---

[52] A husband may not command one of his wives to join and take part in a threesome or command her to watch him perform sex to her co-wife. In *al-Fatawa al-Hindiyya*, 1:341 it has:

"It is unlawful for a man to bring both wives simultaneously in one place even with their consent because this is and leads to utter depravity. If one of the wives brings the other to a single place with consent, it is positively disliked for [the husband] to have sex with one in the presence of the other. And if he commands her to have sex with him, she is not obligated in any way to respond and she will not be considered rebellious for her rejection. There is no disagreement regarding this legal issue."

لَا يَجُوزُ أَنْ يَجْمَعَ بين ضَرَّتَيْنِ أَوْ الضَّرَائِرِ فِي مَسْكَنٍ وَاحِدٍ إلَّا بِرِضَاهُنَّ لِلُزُومِ الْوَحْشَةِ وَلَوْ اجْتَمَعَتْ الضَّرَائِرُ فِي مَسْكَنٍ وَاحِدٍ بِالرِّضَا يُكْرَهُ أَنْ يَطَأَ إحْدَاهُمَا بِحَضْرَةِ الْأُخْرَى حتى لو طَلَبَ وَطْأَهَا لم تَلْزَمْهَا الْإِجَابَةُ وَلَا تَصِيرُ فِي الِامْتِنَاعِ نَاشِزَةً وَلَا خِلَافَ في هذه الْمَسَائِلِ (الفتاوى الهندية، ج 1 ص 341).

[§5.3] Time (*awqat al-jima'* / أوقات الجماع): There is no *shar'i* stipulated time to perform sex.

- Our sacred Law aims to provide solutions to human problems and its rulings are in accordance with what suits and benefits human beings.

- The absence of any specification allows the couples to meet their needs whenever it arises and it also enables them to plan and prepare for that time.

- Although our tradition has a wealth of literature from the noble companions (may Allah be pleased with all of them) as well as statements of the early *Salaf* about when and what is desirable in sex, these are nevertheless non-binding and are based on personal experience and judgment.[53]

- It is not however, unlawful or even prohibitively disliked to engage in full sexual intercourse on Friday as some have suggested. The text of the *hadith* is clear on this issue:

"Whoever bathes himself and causes [his spouse] to bathe on a Friday and then sets out early, walks and does not ride, listens attentively to the Imam in silence, then for every step he will earn the reward of a year's fasting and praying at night."[54]

---

[53] See for example, al-Kawthari, *Islamic Guide to Sexual Relations*, pp.26-34.
[54] Narrated by Aws ibn Abi Aws al-Thaqafi by Tirmidhi in his *Sunan* (#496).

من اغتسل يوم الجمعة وغسل، وبكر وابتكر، ودنا واستمع، وأنصت، كان له بكل خطوة يخطوها أجر سنة صيامها وقيامها

- Imam al-Hafiz Jalal al-Din al-Suyuti (d. 911/1505) gives one of the meanings of "ghassala" ['to cause another to have a bath'] in his commentary on al-Nasa'i's *Sunan*:

"[…] and it is said 'ghassala' means 'to have sex with one's spouse' before going out to [perform the Friday] prayer because it will aid him in lowering his gaze along the way. It is also said the meaning of a man causing his wife to bathe (*ghassala imra'atahu*) with the emphatic vowelling means to have sex with her (*idha jama'aha*)…"[55]

وقيل غسل أي جامع أهله قبل الخروج إلى الصلاة لأنه يعين على غض البصر في الطريق يقال غسل الرجل امرأته بالتخفيف والتشديد إذا جامعها...

(السيوطي، شرح السيوطي على سنن النسائي جـ 3 ص 95 رقم 1381).

- Imam Anwar Shah al-Kashmiri (d. 1933) also gives this as the first meaning in his commentary on the *Sunan* of al-Tirmidhi:

"Regarding his saying ('to cause to bathe'): Waki' said it means to have sex with one's spouse […]."[56]

قوله : (غسل) قال وكيع : مراده أنه جامع (الكشميري، العرف الشذي شرح

---

[55] al-Suyuti, *Sharh Sunan al-Nasa'i*, 3:95.
[56] al-Kashmiri, *al-'Urf al-Shadhy Sharh Sunan al-Tirmidhi*, 2:48. However, he prefers the meaning to be washing the head in agreement with al-Hafiz 'Abd Allah ibn al-Mubarak.

سنن الترمذي جـ 2 ص 48 رقم 496).

- From the above *hadith*, it is inferred that due to the reward in each of the actions mentioned (i.e. 1. Having sex, 2. Bathing, 3. Setting out early for prayer, 4. Walking to the Mosque and 5. Listening attentively to the Imam), one ought to engage in sex with one's partner at least once a week on a Friday.

- Therefore, it would not be contravening the meritorious status or disrespecting the unique excellence of *yawm al-jum'a* by engaging in sex. And Allah knows best.

[§5.4] Frequency of Sex: There is no *shar'i*-specific designated frequency for sex. Islam has left it to the individuals to mutually meet their own sexual requirements.

- However, certain notable *fuqaha'* have designated the frequency of sex which a man ought to engage in with his wife, ranging from:

[1] Once every four nights: this is the advice of Imam al-Ghazzali.[57]

[2] Once every month: this was the view of Imam Ibn Hazm.[58]

[3] Once every four months: this is the opinion of Imam Ibn Qudama.[59]

---

[57] See Ibn 'Abidin, Radd al-Muhtar, 3:203. This was also the opinion of Imam al-Tahawi.
[58] See Ibn Hazm, *al-Muhalla*, p.1672.
[59] See Ibn Qudama, *al-Mughni*, 8:551-552:

[4] Every so often: This is the position of most Hanafi Jurists.

[5] As much as is needed: this is the position of Shaykh al-Islam Ibn Taymiyya.[60]

- Imam Ibn 'Abidin in *Radd al-Muhtar* discusses this issue at length:

"It is mentioned in *al-Fath*: 'know that it is prohibited for [a man] to absolutely stop having sex with [his wife]. Our scholars have clearly explained that it is a religious duty to occasionally or every so often engage in sex with her but it will not be a matter for the courts [s: to enforce it]. Court decree only holds once and they did not designate a period of time or amount. He must not exceed the period of time except with her consent and to make herself feel better.' In *al-Nahr* [*al-Fa'iq*] regarding this discussion, it states that: 'this is clear that performing sex after the first time is his right and not her right.' I say: this is problematic. Rather, it is both his right and her right as well and I understand this to be the case from the fact that it is a religious duty [...] and in

---

إذا كانت له امرأة لزمه المبيت عندها ليلة من كل أربع ليال ما لم يكن له عذر (ابن قدامة، المغني، ج 8 ص 551–552)

[60] Ibn Taymiyya: "A husband is obligated to have sex with his wife as much as is sufficient for her as long as it does not harm his body or occupy him from his other duties…"

ويجب على الزوج وطء امرأته بقدر كفايتها ما لم ينهك بدنه أو يشغله عن معيشته، .. فإن تنازعا فينبغي أن يفرضه الحاكم كالنفقة وكوطئه إذا زاد (الاختيارات الفقهية من فتاوى شيخ الإسلام ابن تيمية ص 246)

al-Bada'i' [*al-Sana'i'*] it has: 'she has a right to demand sex from him because she has a right to derive sexual pleasure from him just as he has the right to derive sexual pleasure from her. If she demands sex, he will be obligated to agree and will be compelled by the courts once only and anything more being considered his religious duty and not a matter for the courts according to some of our scholars whereas others held that it is a matter for the courts'[61] [...] In *al-Fath* it has: as for a man who has only one wife and busies himself in devotion at night neglecting her, al-Tahawi from a narration from al-Hasan [al-Shaybani] from Abu Hanifa was of the opinion that she has a right for a day or night in every four nights and he has the rest of the nights for himself. This is because he has the right to defer her right for three nights due to his being able to marry three other women... However, the established position of the Hanafi School is that no specific stipulation of time may be made...rather he is ordered to spend the night with [his wife] and be in her company every so often without designating a specific time or limit. It was also mentioned in *al-Nahr* from *al-Bada'i'* that what was reported by al-Hasan from Abu Hanifa was his original opinion which he later retracted and so it counts for nothing..."[62]

[...] قال في الفتح واعلم أن ترك جماعها مطلقا لا يحل له صرح أصحابنا بأن جماعها أحيانا واجب ديانة لكن لا يدخل تحت القضاء والإلزام إلا الوطأة الأولى ولم يقدروا فيه مدة ويجب أن لا يبلغ به مدة الإيلاء إلا برضاها وطيب نفسها به

---

[61] See al-Kasani, *al-Bada'i' al-Sana'i'*. 2:331.
[62] Ibn 'Abidin, *Radd al-Muhtar*, 3:202-203.

إه

قال في النهر في هذا الكلام تصريح بأن الجماع بعد المرة حقه لا حقها إه قلت فيه نظر بل هو حقه وحقها أيضا لما علمت من أنه واجب ديانة .

قال في البحر وحيث علم أن الوطء لا يدخل تحت القسم فهل هو واجب للزوجة وفي البدائع لها أن تطالبه بالوطء لأن حله لها حقها كما أن حلها له حقه وإذا طالبته يجب عليه ويجبر عليه في الحكم مرة والزيادة تجب ديانة لا في الحكم عند بعض أصحابنا وعند بعضهم عليه في الحكم إه [...] في الفتح فأما إذا لم يكن له إلا امرأة واحدة فتشاغل عنها بالعبادة أو السراري اختار الطحاوي رواية الحسن عن أبي حنيفة أن لها يوما وليلة من كل أربع ليال وباقيها له لأن له أن يسقط حقها في الثلاث بتزوج ثلاث حرائر. وإن كانت الزوجة أمة فلها يوم وليلة في كل سبع .

وظاهر المذهب أن لا يتعين مقدار لأن القسم معنى نسبي وإيجابه طلب إيجاده وهو يتوقف على وجود المنتسبين فلا يطلب قبل تصوره بل يؤمر أن يبيت معها ويصحبها أحيانا من غير توقيت إه

ونقل في النهر عن البدائع أن ما رواه الحسن هو قول الإمام أولا ثم رجع عنه وأنه ليس بشيء... (ابن عابدين، رد المحتار جـ 3 ص 202-203).

- This fourth and fifth position is perhaps the strongest. And Allah knows best.

[§5.5] Sexual Positions (*ishkal al-jima'* / إشكال الجماع): There is no specific prohibition of assuming a sexual position. Islam has left it open for the couples to explore what induces and generates the most pleasure as long as it does not involve direct harm and as long as it is not anal penetration.[63]

---

[63] See for example, al-Shuri, *Tuhfat al-'Arusayn*, pp.144-148.

§6. Menstruation and Sex

———◆———

- Menstruation is the monthly discharge of blood from the uterus of non-pregnant women from puberty to menopause.[64]

- It is **not** permitted for spouses to have sexual intercourse while the woman is in her menstrual period (*hayd*).

- This is expressly forbidden as stated in the Qur'an and the *hadith* of the Messenger of Allah (saw):

{*And they ask you about menstruation. Say: It is an impurity; therefore keep away from the women during the menstrual discharge and do not approach them until they have become clean; then when they have cleansed themselves, approach them as Allah has commanded you; surely Allah loves those who repent [to Him] much, and He loves those who purify themselves*}[65]

Hadith: "Among the Jews when a woman menstruated they did not eat with her, nor did they live with them in their houses; so the Companions of the Prophet (saw) asked the Apostle (saw) about it and Allah (the Most High) revealed: {*And they ask you about menstruation; say it is an impurity, so keep away from women during menstruation…* [2:222]} to the end. The Messenger of Allah (may peace be upon

---

[64] For detailed rulings on menstruation, see *Introducing the Fiqh of Tahara* (vol.1) by this author as part of the Ad-Duha educational publication series.
[65] Q. 2:222.

him) said: '**Do everything except intercourse**'..."[66]

أن اليهود كانوا ، إذا حاضت المرأة فيهم ، لم يؤاكلوها ولم يجامعوهن في البيوت . فسأل أصحاب النبي صلى الله عليه وسلم النبي صلى الله عليه وسلم . فأنزل الله تعالى : { ويسألونك عن المحيض قل هو أذى فاعتزلوا النساء في المحيض إلى آخر الآية } فقال رسول الله صلى الله عليه وسلم " اصنعوا كل شيء إلا النكاح ..."

- While in her menstruation period, a husband:

    1. May not touch, kiss or arouse his wife in and around the vagina.

    2. May not penetrate or insert any object (e.g. finger, sexual toy, etc.) in the vagina.

    3. May not touch, kiss, arouse or penetrate the anal area.

- However, it is permitted for spouses to enjoy each other as long as it is not within the wife's area encompassing her navel to her knees.

- Thus, the chest, neck, ([face [mouth, lips]), arms, legs and feet are all areas of the wife a husband may derive pleasure from.

- In *al-Fatawa al-Hindiyya* it states:

"And one of the prohibitions is sexual intercourse as mentioned in *al-Nihaya* and *al-Kifaya*. [A husband] may kiss [his wife], lie down with her and derive pleasure from her entire body except what is between

---

[66] Narrated by Anas Ibn Malik by Bukhari in his *Sahih* (#302).

the navel and the knees according to Abu Hanifa and Abu Yusuf as mentioned in al-*Siraj al-Wahhaj*..."[67]

وَمِنْهَا حُرْمَةُ الْجِمَاعِ هَكَذَا فِي النِّهَايَةِ وَالْكِفَايَةِ وَلَهُ أَنْ يُقَبِّلَهَا وَيُضَاجِعَهَا وَيَسْتَمْتِعَ بِجَمِيعِ بَدَنِهَا مَا خَلَا مَا بَيْنَ السُّرَّةِ وَالرُّكْبَةِ عِنْدَ أَبِي حَنِيفَةَ وَأَبِي يُوسُفَ هَكَذَا فِي السِّرَاجِ الْوَهَّاجِ (الفتاوى الهندية، ج 1 ص 39).

- Imam Ibn 'Abidin mentions:

"It is permitted to derive pleasure from the navel and any area above it and the knees and area below it even without a barrier [s: or some sort of covering]. The same is the case even with a barrier where no sexual intercourse takes place and blood comes out..."[68]

فَيَجُوزُ الِاسْتِمْتَاعُ بِالسُّرَّةِ وَمَا فَوْقَهَا وَالرُّكْبَةِ وَمَا تَحْتَهَا وَلَوْ بِلَا حَائِلٍ، وَكَذَا بِمَا بَيْنَهُمَا بِحَائِلٍ بِغَيْرِ الْوَطْءِ وَلَوْ تَلَطَّخَ دَمًا (ابن عابدين، رد المحتار ج 1 ص 292).

- Imam al-Shurunbulali (d. 1069/1659) states:

"...as well as deriving pleasure from whatever is below the navel up to the knees..."[69]

و الاستمتاع بما تحت السرة الى تحت الركبة ... (الشرنبلالي، نور الإيضاح ص

---

[67] See *al-Fatawa al-Hindiyya*, 1:39.
[68] See Ibn 'Abidin, *Radd al-Muhtar*, 1:292. The preposition *ma* / ما here denotes generality ('*umum*) meaning all areas without restriction.
[69] al-Shurunbulali, *Nur al-Idah*, p.49.

.(**49**

- Thus, from the above, we can present the basic rulings within this section as follows:

Permitted:

- Kissing.
- Touching.
- Caressing.
- Fondling.
- Embracing.
- Any form of intimate and sensual contact related to the above.

Prohibited:

- Husband kissing, touching, arousing or penetrating the vagina.
- Masturbating the wife.
- Direct male skin contact with female skin in the area encompassing the woman's navel to her knees.

What spouses can do to each Other

- Both can rub their private parts against each other so long as there is a barrier (*ha'il*) between.
- Wife can masturbate the husband (with hands, feet, breast, etc.).
- Wife can caress and kiss husband all over.
- Husband can kiss wife's legs, feet, neck, cheeks, lips; husband can caress and fondle wife's breasts, etc.

- The same rulings regarding menstruation hold equally for the woman in post-natal bleeding (*al-nifas*).

§7. Anal Sex

──◆──

- **Anal sex** is the sex act of inserting the penis into the anus of another person. It is categorically forbidden to perform anal sex. There is no disagreement over this amongst our *fuqha'*.

- There are numerous *hadith* regarding its prohibition:[70]

Hadith 1: "Allah will not look at a man who enters another man or enters a woman through the anus…"[71]

لا ينظر الله إلى رجل أتى رجلا أو امرأة في الدبر

Hadith 2: "Cursed is the one who enters his wife through the anus…"[72]

ملعون من أتى امرأته في دبرها

Hadith 3: "[…] do not approach woman in their backsides and another time he said 'in their anuses'…"[73]

---

[70] For a discussion, see al-Tijani, *Tuhfat al-'Arus wa Mut'at al-Nufus*, pp.385; al-Tahir, *Tuhfat al-'Arus*, pp.200-202 and al-Shu'aysha', *Tuhfat al-'Arus*, pp.164-171.
[71] Narrated by Ibn 'Abbas by Tirmidhi, *Sunan* (#1165). See also al-Tahawi, *Sharh Ma'ani al-Athar*, 3:44; al-Hafiz Ibn Hajar al-'Asqalani, *Hidayat al-Ruwat*, 3:279 (#3131) and al-Shawkani, *Nayl al-Awtar*, 6:352.
[72] Narrated by Abu Hurayra by Abu Dawud in his *Sunan* (#2155 & 2162) and Ahmad in the *Musnad*, 2/479.
[73] Narrated by 'Ali ibn Abi Talib as evaluated by al-Haythami in *Majma' al-Zawa'id*, 1:248.

ولا تأتوا النساء في أعجازهن وقال مرة في أدبارهن

Hadith 4: "…Allah is not ashamed of the Truth. Do not enter women in their anus."[74]

استحيوا فإن الله لا يستحي من الحق ولا تأتوا النساء في أدبارهن

Hadith 5: "Whoever enters a menstruating woman or a woman in her anus has disbelieved in what was revealed to Muhammad."[75]

من أتى حائضا أو امرأة في دبرها فقد كفر بما أنزل على محمد

- The contextual indications (*qara'in*) from these narrations are decisive (*qat'i*): [1] Allah not looking at a person indicates His wrath; this is an indication that a matter is unlawful (*haram*); [2] being described with Allah and His Messenger's curse is another indication that a matter is unlawful and [3] being described with *kufr* ('ingratitude', 'disbelief') is also an incontrovertible indication that a particular matter is unlawful.[76]

---

[74] Narrated by 'Umar as evaluated by al-Haythami in *Majma' al-Zawa'id*, 4:301.

[75] Narrated by Abu Hurayra by Abu Dawud in his *Sunan* (#135). See also Ibn al-'Arabi, *'Aridat al-Ahwadhi*, 1:188.

[76] For a discussion of contextual indications (*qara'in*) within *usul al-fiqh*, refer to Shaykh 'Ata' ibn Khalil's chapter *Taysir al-Wusul ila'l-Usul*, pp.19-29. The reference to 'kufr' in the *hadith* suggests the severity of the action although if one actually believes they are permitted after being shown the evidences to the contrary, he would be committing disbelief. Imam al-Mubarakpuri in *Tuhfat al-Ahwadhi*, 1:448 states:

§8. Miscellaneous Rulings

──── ♦ ────

- **Sex and *Qibla* direction**: some of the scholars have ruled it is disliked out of veneration for the Sacred House. Others have ruled with permissibility.

- **Sex on the first night of marriage**: it is not mandatory to have sex on the first night of the marriage (*laylat al-zufaf*). Couples should engage in intimate contact only when they feel comfortable.

- **Sex in the bathroom**: it is permissible but disliked due to the scenario of having to recite the supplication upon ejaculation and Allah's name mentioned in a toilet or bathroom is not proper and hence disliked.

- **Bath after sex**: it is recommended to perform a full ritual bath (*ghusl*) immediately after sex

---

"[...] and the meaning of this *hadith* according to the people of knowledge is that it indicates severity [...] (**He has disbelieved in what was revealed to Muhammad**). Its apparent meaning is severity and strong censure as al-Tirmidhi mentioned. It is also said to mean that if one enters [s: his wife while in menstruation or through the anus] believing it to be permitted and is convinced of it then he has disbelieved based on the apparent meaning. Other than these two [s: apparent meanings], it is considered a disbelief of ingratitude (*kufran al-ni'ma*)."

وَإِنَّمَا مَعْنَى هَذَا عِنْدَ أَهْلِ العِلمِ عَلَى التَّغْلِيظِ... (فقد كفر بما أنزل على محمد) الظاهر أنه محمول على التغليظ والتشديد كما قاله الترمذي وقيل إن كان المراد الإتيان باستحلال وتصديق فالكفر محمول على ظاهره وإن كان بدونهما فهو على كفران النعمة (المباركفوري، تحفة الأحوذي جـ 1 ص 448).

although it is permitted to remain in a state of ritual impurity until before Fajr time.

- **Repeated sex**: there is no prohibition on the number of times spouses engage in sexual activity during the day or night. It is up to them to decide what is most comfortable and feasible.

- **Divulging sexual matters**: it is prohibited to divulge or discuss one's private sexual matters. This includes sexual secrets. The exception is in cases of necessity or need, e.g. religious counseling, medical reports, etc. but the detail must be as minimum as possible.

- **Refusing sex**: It is not permissible for a wife to refuse sex with her husband unless there is a Shariah reason (e.g. illness, emergency, menstruation, recovery, etc.). This is not a permission to sexually assault or oppress his wife. A husband too should not neglect the needs of his wife and continually doing so would be held as contempt of her marital right.

- **Sex and pornography**: It is not permitted to watch pornographic films for stimulation because watching these films are totally against Islamic culture and standards of moral decency. Also, it is prohibited to look at nudity.

- **Sex and pregnancy**: it is permitted for spouses to have sex during the pregnancy term if there is no medical restriction or prohibition (e.g. harmful to the mother, etc.).

- **Sex and getaways**: it is permitted for couples to romance each other with quick breaks on the weekends or short holidays in order to build intimacy.

- **Sex and condoms**: it is permitted to use contraceptive methods like condoms.

§9. Conclusion

──── ♦ ────

- The above volume is a very small and humble attempt to outline some of the 'bedroom fiqh' from the Holy Qur'an, noble *hadith* and luminous works of the Hanafi *fuqaha'*.

- Contrary to popular assumptions and understandings, Islam's realm of permissibility afforded to the spouses is indeed great.

- With the exception of a few injunctions, there is great latitude for enhancing – as well as increasing and intensifying in love, sensuality and physical enjoyment – the relationship of marriage.

- The books of *fiqh* ('knowledge of Islamic Law') treat this subject matter with a required balance and detail. Islam is a comprehensive religion with rulings from the Quran and *Sunna* in **all** areas of life and marital relations are no exceptions.

- Of course, due to decorum and a strong sense of modesty, these rulings from our Sacred Law are not made easily accessible to public readership.

- Another factor for the inaccessibility is the lack of translation of the classical Islamic material for these issues in English. Thus, it is hoped that this small work has redressed this lack somewhat.

- I ask Allah Almighty to accept this humble effort by one in most need of His help and one in most need of reminder.

Abundant blessings and peace upon our Master, the best of creation, the *nur* of Guidance, our Beloved, the Messenger of Allah (saw), his pure family and noble Companions. *Amin.*

[End].

S. Z. Chowdhury,
London 2008 (updated).

Appendix:
Etiquettes on the Wedding Night
(آداب ليلة الزفاف)

──── ♦ ────

- Indeed, the wedding night is often a daunting but also exciting moment for newly-weds. It is considered to be an extremely important night as it determines in some large part the subsequent impression of the intimate aspects of marital relationship. As with all aspects of life, Islam too has guidelines for conducting this night.

- Below are some of these etiquettes (*adab*) taken from the blessed narrations of the Prophet (saw) so that by emulating them spouses can begin on the strongest footing for their private life.

Etiquette 1: to make the wife feel at ease and relaxed by being kind to her such as offering something to drink. This is based on the *hadith* of Asma' bint Yazid Ibn al-Sakan who said:

I beautified 'A'isha for Allah's Messenger, then called him to come to see her unveiled. He came, sat next to her and brought a large cup of milk from which he drank. Then, he offered it to A'isha, but she lowered her head and felt shy. I scolded her and said to her: 'Take from the hand of the Prophet.' She then took it and drank some. Then, the Prophet said to her: **"Give some to your companion."** At that point, I said: 'O Messenger of Allah, rather take it yourself and drink and then give it to me from your hand.' He took it, drank some, and then offered it to me. I sat down and put it on my knees. Then, I began rotating it and following it with my lips in order that I might hit the spot from which the Prophet had drank. Then, the Prophet said about some women who were there with me: **"Give them some."** But, they said: 'We don't want it.' (i.e. we are not hungry). The Prophet said: **"Do not combine hunger and fibbing!"**[77]

إني قيّنت عائشة لرسول الله صلى الله عليه وسلم، ثم جئته فدعوته لجلوتها، فجاء، فجلس إلى جنبها، فأتي بعُس لبن، فشرب، ثم ناولها النبي صلى الله عليه وسلم فخضت رأسها واستحيت، قالت أسماء: فانتهرتها، وقلت لها: خذي من يد النبي صلى الله عليه وسلم، قالت: فأخذت، فشربت شيئاً، ثم قال لها النبي صلى الله عليه وسلم: أعطي تربك، قالت أسماء: فقلت: يا رسول الله! بل خذه فاشرب منه ثم ناولنيه من يدك، فأخذه فشرب منه ثم ناولنيه، قالت: فجلست، ثم وضعته على ركبتي، ثم طفقت أديره وأتبعه بشفتي لأصيب منه شرب النبي صلى الله عليه وسلم، ثم قال لنسوة عندي: ناوليهن، فقلن: لا نشتيه! فقال صلى الله عليه وسلم: لا تجمعن جوعاً وكذباً

- This is to make one's spouse feel relaxed.
- This is to help one's spouse overcome any nervousness or anxiety.
- This is also a way to build communication and ease any visible tension.

Etiquette 2: to hold the wife's forelock (front part of the head) and offer the following supplication as recorded in the *hadith*: "When any of you marries a woman ... he should hold her forelock, mention Allah Most High and pray for His blessings saying:

O Allah, I ask You for the good in her and the good with which You have created her; and I seek refuge in

---

[77] Ahmad, *al-Musnad*, 6/438, 452-3 and 458.

You from the evil in her and the evil with which You have created her.[78]

إذا تزوج أحدكم امرأةً، أو اشترى خادماً، [فليأخذ بناصيتها]، [وليسم الله عز وجل]، [وليدع بالبركة]، وليقل:

اللهم إني أسألك من خيرها وخير ما جبلتها عليه، وأعوذ بك من شرّها وشر ما جبلتها عليه.

- This is in order to seek protection from Allah.
- This is to begin one's intimate moment seeking Allah's help and succor from satanic whisperings.
- The wife may also supplicate to Allah in the same emanner.

Etiquette 3: Both spouses should offer 2 units (*rak'a*) prayers – preferably in congregation (with the woman behind the husband). Throughout the night, it is also preferable to offer the prayer of thanks (*shukr*), need (*haja*) and the night-vigil prayer (*tahajjud*). These are based on the following narrations:

[1] Abu Sa'id client (*mawla*) of Abu Usayd who said: "I got married while I was a slave. I invited a number of the companions of the Prophet, among them was Ibn Mas'ud, Abu Dharr and Hudhayfa. When the prayer was called, Abu Dharr began to step forward when the others said to him: 'No!' He said: 'Is it so?' And they said: 'Yes.' Then, I stepped forward and led the prayer though I was a slave. They taught me,

---

[78] Abu Dawud, *Sunan* (#2153) from which the wording of the supplication is taken. See also, Bukhari, *Khalq Af'al al-'Ibad*, p.22.

saying: 'When your wife comes to you, pray two *rak'a* (units). Then, ask Allah for the good of that which has come to you and seek refuge in Him from its evil. Then it is up to you and it is up to your wife.'[79]

تزوجت وأنا مملوك، فدعوت نفراً من أصحاب النبي صلى الله عليه وسلم فيهم ابن مسعود وأبو ذر وحذيفة، قال: وأقيمت الصلاة، قال: فذهب أبو ذر ليتقدم، فقالوا: إليك! قال: أو كذلك؟ قالوا: نعم، قال: فتقدمت بهم وأنا عبد مملوك، وعلموني فقالوا: إذا دخل عليك أهلك فصل ركعتين، ثم سل الله من خير ما دخل عليك، وتعوذ به من شره، ثم شأنك وشأن أهلك

[2] From Shaqiq who related that: a man named Abu Hariz came to 'Abd Allah Ibn Mas'ud and said: 'I have married a young girl and I am afraid that she will despise me'. 'Abd Allah ibn Mas'ud said to him: 'Verily, closeness is from Allah and hatred is from Shaytan, who wishes to make despicable that which Allah has allowed. So, when your wife comes to you, tell her to pray behind you two *rak'a* of prayer.'[80]

جاء رجل يقال له: أبو حريز، فقال: إني تزوجت جارية شابة [بكراً]، وإني أخاف أن تفركني، فقال عبد الله (يعني ابن مسعود): إن الإلف من الله، والفرك من الشيطان، يريد أن يكرّه إليكم ما أحل الله لكم؛ فإذا أتتك فأمرها أن تصلي وراءك ركعتين.

Another version from Ibn Mas'ud (ra) reads: *"O Allah, bless me for my family and bless them for me. O Allah, join us together as long as You join us in good and separate us if you do with good."*[81]

---

[79] al-Tabarani, *al-Mu'jam al-Kabir*, 9:204.
[80] 'Abd al-Razzaq, *al-Musannaf*, 6:83.
[81] *Adab al-Zufaf* of al-Albani, pp.24-25.

اللهم بارك لي في أهلي، وبارك لهم فيّ، اللهم اجمع بيننا ما جمعت بخير؛ وفرق بيننا إذا فرقت إلى خير

- Aside from the above, it may also be advisable:

1. To beautify one's self in order to engender attraction.

2. To use the *miswak* (tooth-stick) in order to freshen the mouth and engender attraction.

3. To not pressure each other to have sex right away but make most of the night to talk and discuss feelings and to reflect on the day.

4. To have a clean and presentable placc.

KEY REFERENCES

Arabic References:

Ibn 'Abidin, *Hashiyat Radd al-Muhtar 'ala 'l-Durr al-Mukhtar Sharh Tanwir al-Absar*, 7 vols. Beirut: Dar al-Ihya' al-Turath al-'Arabi, n.d.

———— *Radd al-Muhtar 'ala 'l-Durr al-Mukhtar*, 8 vols. Karachi: H. M. S. Co., 1986.

al-'Asqalani, *Fath al-Bari Sharh Sahih al-Bukhari* (Baz and `Abd al-Baqi edn.), 15 vols. Beirut: Dar al-Kutub al-'Ilmiyya, 1997.

al-Bahlawi, *Adillat al-Hanafiyya min al-Ahadith al-Nabawiyya 'ala 'l-Masa'il al-Fiqhiyya*, Damascus: Dar al-Qalam, 2007.

al-Haythami, *Majma' al-Zawa'id*, Cairo: Maktbat al-Qudsi, n.d.

———— al-Haythami, *Majma' al-Zawa'id*, Beirut: Dar al-Kitab al-'Arabi, 1982.

Ibn al-Humam, *Fath al-Qadir li 'l-'Ajiz al-Faqir Sharh al-Hidaya*, 9 vols. Beirut: Dar al-Ihya' al-Turath al-'Arabi, 1997.

Ibn al-Jawzi, *Sayd al-Khatir*, Riyad: Dar al-Yaqin, 1993.

———— *Talbis Iblis*, Cairo: Maktabat al-Thaqafi, 2001.

al-Kasani, *al-Bada'i' al-Sana'i' fi Tartib al-Shara'i'*, 6 vols. Beirut: Dar al-Ihya' al-Turath al-'Arabi, 2000.

al-Marghinani, *al-Hidaya Sharh Bidyat al-Mubtadi*, 4 vols. Beirut: Dar al-Kutub al-'Ilmiyya, 2000.

Mawlana Nizam, et al. *al-Fatawa al-Hindiyya*, 6 vols. Quetta: Maktaba Majdiyya, 1983.

――――――― *al-Fatawa al-Hindiyya*, repr. Beirut: Dar al-Fikr, 1979.

――――――― *al-Fatawa al-Hindiyya*, 6 vols. Beirut: Dar Ihya' Turath al-'Arabi, 1980.

al-Mawsili, *Kitab al-Ikhtiyar li-Ta'lil al-Mukhtar*, 5 vols. Cairo: Dar al-Ma'rifa, 2000.

al-Maydani, *al-Lubab fi Sharh al-Kitab*, 4 vols. Karachi: Kutub Khana, n.d.

al-Nawawi, *Sharh Sahih Muslim*, 18 vols. Beirut: Dar Ihya' al-Turath al-'Arabi,1972.

al-Nadwi, S. al-*Fiqh al-Muyassar*, Karachi: Zam-Zam Publications, 2009.

Ibn Nujaym, *al-Bahr al-Ra'iq fi Sharh Kanz al-Daqa'iq*, 9 vols. Beirut: Dar al-Kutub al-'Ilmiyya, 1997.

Qudri Paşa, *al-Ahkam al-Shari'iyyah fi 'l-Ahwal al-Shakhsiyyah*, Cairo, 1924.

al-Qal'aji, M. et al, *Mu'jam al-Lughat al-Fuqaha'*, Beirut: Dar al-Nafa'is, 2000.

al-Quduri, *al-Mukhtasar* (English-Arabic text, trans. M. Kiani, London: Dar al-Taqwa, 2009).

al-Shurunbulali, *Nur al-Idah* (English-Arabic text, trans. W. Charkawi) n.p. 2004.

——— *Maraqi al-Falah Sharh Nur al-Idah*, Damascus: Maktabat al-'Ilm al-Hadith, 2001.

——— *Maraqi al-Falah Sharh Nur al-Idah*, Beirut: Dar al-Kutub al-'Ilmiyya, 1995.

——— *Imdad al-Fattah Sharh Nur al-Idah*, Damascus, n.p. 2001.

——— *Maraqi al-Sa'adat*, Beirut: Dar al-Kutub al-Lubnani, 1973 and English trans. by F. A. Khan, London: Whitethread Press, 2010.

——— *Sabil al-Falah fi Sharh Nur al-Idah*, Beirut: Dar al-Bayruti, n.d.

Usmani, M. T. *Takmilat Fath al-Mulhim*, 3 vols. Karachi: Maktabat-i Dar al-'Ulum, 1986-1987.

Urdu References:

Khan, Ahmed Reza. *al-'Ataya li-Nabawiyya fi' l-Fatawa al-Ridwiyya*, 6 vols. Mubarakpur: Sunni Darul Isha'at, 1981.

——— *al-'Ataya al-Nabawiyya fi' l-Fatawa al-Ridwiyya*, 12 vols. Faisalabad: Maktaba Nuriyya Ridwiyya.

Ludhianvi, Rashid Ahmad. *Ahsan al-Fatawa*, Karachi: H. M. S. Co, 1398–.

Usmani, 'Aziz al-Rahman. *'Aziz al-Fatawa*, Karachi: Darul Isha'at, n.d.

―――― '*Aziz al-Fatawa*, 2 vols. Deoband Fatwa Department, n.d.

English References:

Ghazali, A. H. *The Proper Conduct of Marriage in Islam* (*adab al-nikah*), tr. Muhtar Holland, al-Baz Publishing, 1998.

al-Jibaly, M. *Closer than a Garment: Marital Intimacy According to the Pure Sunnah*, London: al-Kitab, 2006.

al-Kawthari, M. *Islamic Guide to Sexual Relations, Huma Press*, 2008.

Thanwi, A. A. *The Islamic Marriage*, Karachi: Darul Isha'at, 2004.

Notes

Other Titles

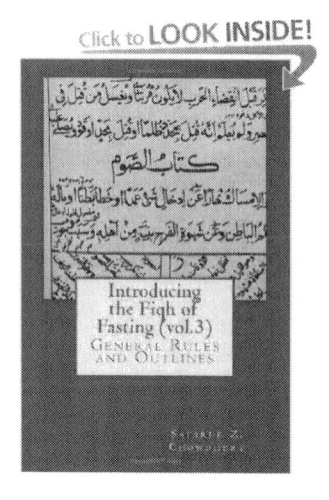

S. Z. Chowdhury, *Introducing the Fiqh of Fasting* (vol.3)

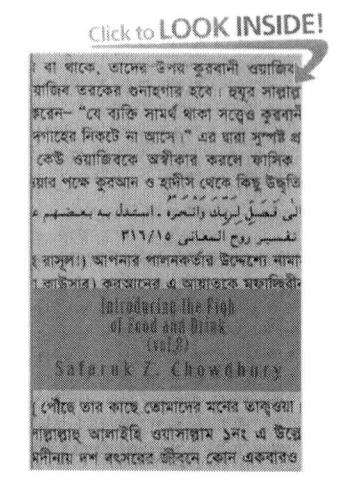

S. Z. Chowdhury, **Introducing the Fiqh of Food and Drink (vol.8)**

S. Z. Chowdhury, *Introducing the Fiqh of Zaka*t (vol.4)

S. Z. Chowdhury, *Introducing the Fiqh of Employment* (vol.10)

S. Z. Chowdhury, *Introducing the Fiqh of Marriage and Divorce* (vol.6)

Printed in Great Britain
by Amazon.co.uk, Ltd.,
Marston Gate.